Beauty For Ashes

VOLUME II

Dr. LaMonica Abner

This book is the personal testimony of the author and has been composed from the recollection of the events of her life. Some names and places have been changed to protect identities and details.

clfpublishing.org
909.315.3161

Cover design by Senir Design. Contact info: info@senirdesign.com

ISBN #978-1-945102-98-1

Dedications

To the little girl in me
and to all the little girls who are just like me.

To all the teenage moms out there!

To all the millions of people who are dealing with some sort of childhood trauma that shaped your future and you feel as though you cannot or will not be anything in life.

I want you to know your pain is real! What you went through is real! And, you will one day recover from what or who hurt you in life if you allow God to be with you in your change.

Special Thanks

To God my Father in heaven, you have been the only consistent thing in my life even when I did not know you were there all along. You are my God, my Father, my keeper, my protector, my friend, my whatever I needed you to be at the moment. Thank you, my Creator!

To my dad, Terece LaMont Hart; my mom, Belinda Carter; my big brother, De-Shawn Cunningham (He will always be in my heart.); my little brother, Charles V. Carter; my grandmother, Vernell Walker (I really wish she could have seen this day.); my uncles and my aunt Adrienne Hobbs, who always accepted me no matter what went on in my life. She always told me things would change.

To everyone who has been in my life, who said a prayer for me, who sat and talked with me for hours, who sat and took my calls late in the midnight hours, to all the ones who said I would not be anything, who did not believe in me, who said I was not anointed and did not believe God could turn my life around. Thank you because it kept me in the face of God. And, He truly turned my ashes into beauty!

To my seven! Rodric J. Harris Jr., Ra'Shawn D. Shearin, Tyonna R. Davis (Scutter), Tyliah M. Davis, Tyden J. Davis, Jaelle M. Davis, and Josiah K. Abner. If it were not for you all, life would not be the same. God saw fit to allow me to have you all. Even though I might not have always been the best teen mom, God threw me a lifeline, and it was you all. And for that, I want to say thank you, God for all seven of my blessings!

To my publisher, Dr. C. White-Elliott, at CLF Publishing, LLC. If it were not for you, I would not have been able to share my story.

Faith Walk Bookstore - The Diggins
20411 S. Susana Rd. Long Beach, CA 90810

FOREWORD
by Evangelist Mrs. Linda L. Burney, MA Ed.

Dr. Abner's debut book, *Beauty for Ashes*, is not a 'rags-to-riches' fairy tale that panders to the reader's fancy. Neither is it just another "how to" manual. It is the true, unvarnished, autobiography of a young woman's journey of redemption, resilience, endurance, and grace. It's about the grit and self-determination that guided her from the uncertainties of her pre-teen years through the confusing mazes of her spotted adulthood.

The graphic stories come from the unpleasant, but sacred spaces of her reality, many of which I have heard first-hand from her own lips. She and I have laughed together and we have cried together. Having spent time with her as a neighbor, I knew that God had a plan for her life. More importantly, SHE knew that God had a plan for her life. And this work describes in vivid and glaring detail how that plan is yet unfolding, step by miraculous step.

The book tells how the seed of God's Word planted in the fertile soil of a child's battered and bruised heart was destined to one day bloom into a sanctuary of hope for other broken souls. Beauty for Ashes actually takes the reader on a journey of stark realism where well-crafted vignettes not only spotlight the villains who lurked in all the pathways of LaMonica's life, they also showcase the truths that exposed them.

You will literally wince at the clamorous sounds and scenes created by cleverly selected words as well as clap for the victories of unlikely heroes and heroines. For certain, all who read this book will crescendo in praise to the God of the Bible who still promises a future and a hope to those who dare to place their trust in Him (Jeremiah 29:11, KJV).

Beauty for Ashes is a must read and highly recommended for anyone facing life's toughest challenges.

FOREWORD
by Dr. C. White-Elliott

Beauty for Ashes, an autobiographical account of Dr. LaMonica Abner's life, is a testament to the awesome, majestic power of the Holy Spirit. In the midst of a tale of woes, a tale of hope and perseverance is embedded. Riding her personal roller coaster of life, LaMonica was thrown from one devastating ordeal to another, while tightly holding on as though her very life depended upon it. Quite frankly, it did. Thankfully, the trials and tests were unable to deter her nor cause her to falter. Rather, they strengthened her resolve, leaving her clinging to unshakeable and undeniable hope as well as blind faith in the Creator.

If you or someone you know wants to witness the miraculous working power of Almighty God, peruse the pages of her journey. Therein lies a formidable young woman who knows not her destiny. Despite being underprepared for the impending challenges she would inevitably face, she faithfully places her life and the lives of her children in the hands of the Master. Just as Dr. Abner, with her faith tested to unspeakable limits, found God to be true to His Word as the omnipotent, omnipresent, and omniscient One, you will too.

Volume One begins her journey, but by no means does it detail her entire life's encounters. After you have perused and ingested the contents of *Beauty for Ashes Volume One*, continue to follow Dr. Abner's journey in the upcoming volumes, reading until her journey culminates.

FOREWORD
by Pastor Jason Malveaux

Pastor LaMonica Abner and I have known one another for several years working vocationally in ministry. I know her to be a dedicated inner-city servant. She is one who is unafraid, unmoved, and unbothered by the streets of Los Angeles. Whether doing outreach to the homeless, spiritual warfare conferences, or Sunday Worship in Gonzalez Park, she is moved to place the Gospel front and center for those who are in obvious need of its message.

Beauty for Ashes, the appropriate title of this book, is very much the autobiographical account of Pastor LaMonica's extraordinary life experience and walk with God. An artist's rendering of a bowl of fruit, a starry night, or an ordinary woman has survived the centuries as works of art and hold their place in the earthen pantheon of the extraordinary. What is extraordinary about Lamonica Abner is she chose the cathartic journey of placing her life in a book. Hundreds of years from now, in an obscure library, a student or suffering soul will be looking for answers and be drawn to Beauty for Ashes.

Beauty for Ashes will not tell the story of a woman educated in elite universities, whose trajectory was incompatible with ordinary human beings. Quite the contrary, *Beauty for Ashes* will tell the extraordinary story of an ordinary human being who traversed pain, guilt, suffering, grief, and loss experiencing both success and failure while holding fast to the unchanging hand of God. The extraordinary thing about Pastor Lamonica Abner's story is just how ordinary it is for our time.

As of this writing, The National Center for Victims of Crime, reports that 1 in 5 girls between the ages of 14 and 17 experience molestation. Certainly, the circumstance of being molested is extraordinarily heinous, but the fact is that its frequency makes it ordinary in our society. What a sad commentary! But, Pastor Lamonica Abner, with the help of our Lord and Savior Jesus Christ, found a way to find safety in her relationship with God, through Christ Jesus.

The Center for Disease Control and Prevention tracks the U.S. marriage and divorce rate per thousand citizens in the U.S. Population. Furthermore, they issued a report called "The National Marriage and Divorce Rate Trends of 2000-2020." The report suggests that 45% +/-5% of all marriages are ending in divorce. Divorce is an extraordinarily painful experience to suffer. Pastor Lamonica knows all too well, having negotiated this territory twice, the mental, emotional, and spiritual hardship that divorce brings to one's life. Rather than keep it quiet, rather than save herself the embarrassment of discussing it openly, she has chosen to bravely open her extraordinary life to us.

Pastor Timothy Ross of the Embassy Church in Houston Texas says in his podcast "your vulnerability is a gift." If for no other reason than fellowship, this book is worth reading. Fellowship is not merely spending time in the same room sharing pleasantries. Rather, it is spending time in someone else's space and sharing each other's experiences. Such a sharing of experience creates community, fosters belonging, and solidifies the message to the soul that you are not alone. And so for the reader, whose life is scarred by extraordinary suffering, let us gather together in Pastor LaMonica Abner's story and let God give you Beauty for Ashes.

Table of Contents

Volume I Recap

Prologue
A Moment in Time

Have you ever experienced your life spinning around in circles as though a tornado or whirlwind was circling around you? Did you feel as though your life was topsy-turvy and everything was going downhill quickly? That was the experience I had during the months of April to June of 2010.

Inside a crowded courtroom, the effects of the whirlwind can be felt by all parties involved: those in support of the defense; those in support of the prosecution; and onlookers who have yet to make up their minds. In April of 2010, the whirlwind landed the accused in the Clark Superior Court in New Jersey. Those on the side of the defense were many, and they staunchly supported the defendant and prayed for his acquittal. In contrast, those on the side of the prosecution were few in number, and they desperately wanted justice to be served. For the duration of the events that led to the proceedings and the proceedings themselves, those who sided with the prosecution were inundated with despair, hurt, helplessness, fear, and frustration.

On that day in April, all parties had their eyes trained on 19-year-old Rodolfo Ramirez, who stood before the crowded courtroom. Ramirez was on trial for committing heinous crimes. No one, absolutely no one, could side with Ramirez by directly agreeing with what he had been accused. At the same time though, Ramirez's family and some of the church members were there to demonstrate their support of forgiving Ramirez's "mistake," because he exhibited repentance and was known to be a nice guy.

In this twisted, unfortunate, life-altering sequence of events, the presiding judge made his ruling as all the onlookers held their breath in anticipation.

Chapter One Closing Thought

In the midst of all the turbulence my family and I were experiencing with all the unsettling circumstances of abuse and death, there were a few shining moments. One was a shining moment of red. Uncle Lonnie surprised me with a bright red ten-speed bicycle. I was very excited because that was my first bike ever, and it was beautiful. Prior to that, the only 'vehicle' I had owned had been a Big Wheel when I was a little kid. I rode my bike all throughout the neighborhood with a large grin spread across my face. But, it did not take too long before I got a flat tire. After that, I never rode the bike again. It was fun while it lasted.

Chapter Two Closing Thought

Within the next week, I applied for welfare, as I needed to secure income for myself. While waiting for my first check, I stayed with my uncle and his family for about a month and a half. Meanwhile, I focused on figuring out where I would live once I left their home. Having many conversations with my friend Cindy, we decided to get an apartment together. Having a place to call my own was very appealing. That meant I would be making a permanent move back to New Jersey. So, when I received my first welfare check, I purchased a one-way airline ticket, packed my bags, and off I went.

Chapter Three Closing Thought

With my son's father being absent from my son's life, I made it my sole pursuit to do my very best in raising him alone. In my efforts to nurture my son and give him the best life possible, I vowed to not be the type of parent my mom had been. In my desire to be different, I became overprotective. I would not let anyone touch him, and I did not want to leave him with a babysitter. When I was asked to go to the club, I responded, "I can't leave my baby." Eventually, I did leave him with someone I trusted. She was the person whom I considered to be a sister. Everyone thought we actually were sisters because she looked my mother. It was her ID I used to get into the clubs. The few times I left him with her, I would go directly back to pick him up when I left the club. He was my baby, and I vowed to protect him at all costs. Finally, I had someone to love and to love me back.

Chapter Four Closing Thought

On one particular afternoon, I needed to go to the market to pick up a few items for dinner, but I did not want to take my children with me. I knew I could get there faster if I were alone. So, I asked a woman from my church, who lived in the same complex, if her son, who was a teenager, could watch the boys for me for just a short time. She said yes, and he came over to my apartment. I was gone for about twenty-five minutes, and as soon as I got back to the apartment with the groceries, the teenage boy put his shoes on and ran out of the door very quickly and right on down the stairs. I looked at him with a look of surprise not understanding why he was so anxious.

1

A Fairytale

I stood there dumbfounded. I had no idea what would make him jump up and run out like that without even saying goodbye. Assuming it was due to his adolescent nature, I shrugged my shoulders as if to say, "I am clueless about that..." At that point, there was nothing else to do but move on with my evening, so I began to unload the bags of groceries I had purchased at the market. Then, I shifted by attention to my sons; my baby boy (who was six months) was lying on the couch, while my two year old was playing as he sat on the floor. After unloading the bags, I prepared dinner, which was my usual evening pastime.

After dinner had been eaten and my oldest son had a little tv time, I settled both boys into their beds in their room, and I retired into my room. I was really enjoying our new apartment. It had not been too long since we had moved from our one-bedroom apartment across the hall to the larger two-bedroom unit. That gave me a little privacy from the boys, which I did not hesitate to enjoy from time to time, the first time being on moving day.

On that day, I only had one person assist me with the move because my circle of friends had begun to dwindle down to just a select few as I separated myself more and more, to focus on myself, my sons, and the Lord. I had increased my faith walk and was spending more time in church than ever before.

The one person who assisted in the move from the old apartment to the new one was a long-time friend. And, in my state of vulnerability and loneliness, we ended up engaging in intercourse that day. I don't really know why I did it, as I was not in a relationship with him. I can only guess that my single state and desire to be with someone took over me. It was a one-time incident and never occurred again.

Despite contending with my one illness of loneliness, I was able to thrive and survive on my own. I maintained a job, which allowed me the comforts of my own apartment to house myself and my children. I also had been able to purchase my own vehicle to transport us wherever we needed to go. Yet, my loneliness caused me to act out in ways I later regretted.

My state of loneliness also caused me to cling to people. For example, I met a very sweet guy, who was actually from my home town, but I did not meet him until I was pregnant with Rod. C was a military man, and we became fast friends. We would hang out together and have a great time. After Rod was born, C continued to hang out with me at my apartment and assist me with taking care of my son. He would warm his bottles in the middle of the night and still get up and go to work the next morning.

Even with his sweet demeanor, I could feel there was something lurking underneath that would soon rear its ugly head. I would see glimpses of it, but one night when we went out dancing, I was able to see his "evil twin" on full display. While we were at the club having a great time, I saw several people I knew and started dancing with one of my best friends, Jace. C blew a fuse! He went off in front of everyone. But, no one was really alarmed. They found the entire situation hilarious. Their laughter only made C angrier. At that point, I guess C felt he had something to prove, so he started portraying a gangbanger persona. That really set everyone's laughter off. They said, "We are over here on an island! What are you doing?" But, C was in his own world.

After that night, I knew I should tread carefully. But, I did not heed what I felt in my spirit. I continued seeing him, but I had reservations, and I'm sure my sense of loneliness propelled me forward and allowed me to keep seeing him.

During our relationship, I left town to go on vacation to California for a month. While I was away, I had a dream that my front door had been kicked in, but I didn't give the dream too much attention. I just kept it in the back of my mind. However, when I returned home, I actually did find my front door kicked in with the door jamb damaged. I immediately went downstairs and asked the manager if she knew anything about it. She said she had heard a disturbance upstairs, but I guess it did not alarm her too much because she did not check out the noise she had heard. There was no information on who caused the damage, but in my spirit I knew C was behind it.

After that, I did not want to give C another opportunity to act out towards me, and I certainly did not want to become a victim of his rage, so I broke things off. I would like to say that was the end of his attention towards me, but unfortunately it was not. He wanted us to be together again, so he did all he could to make me jealous and come back to him. He began dating a young lady who used to live with me. I'm sure he thought that would do the trick of turning my head, but I was done with him, and I was not looking back.

When dating the young woman did not work, he moved into my building in the apartment above Vincent's family. The view from his apartment allowed him to look into the three windows of my apartment. But, I continued to ignore him.

During the same time frame, I had met a Hispanic family, who was part of our church, and the wife and I became good friends. I would frequent her home quite often until I reached the point of going over there every day. I could tell that even though her husband liked me, he did not particularly care for me being in their home every single day. Meanwhile, I was enjoying my friend's company and did not concern myself with her husband's disposition. During our time together, I learned so much from her. She taught me how to cook and be a good wife, so one day when I became a wife I would know what to do.

I took some of what I had learned from her in the kitchen and cooked for my sons, which I loved to do, making sure they had hot, healthy meals each night. Also, I loved spending quality time with my boys. On occasion, I would take them to the beach. One day when we were there enjoying a relaxing day in the sun, I saw two other boys running around playing and having a good time. However, the closer I got to them, I realized the older one was not actually a boy at all. He was a nice-looking young man, who seemed to notice me as well. But, I was sure I looked like a young girl to him because I was wearing a pair of overalls and had my hair in the Janet Jackson style braids, which always has a tendency to make women look younger.

Surprisingly, a week or so later, the young man showed up at my church, but he was not alone. He had a woman by his side. Looking at them briefly, I figured she must have been his girlfriend or his wife. Not wanting to be presumptuous or to appear interested in someone who could have been another woman's man and not trying to look desperate by watching him, I made sure my eyes and attention were turned in another direction. Plus, I knew the other single women would be eyeing him. Furthermore, the other women (married and single) always seemed to assume I was looking for a man. Frankly, they were wrong. That was not my number one agenda.

At that time, I was working at the Exchange, the military department store on base. Although I enjoyed working there, as a single mother and a single woman, I made sure I did not engage the attention of the Black men because I never knew where their minds were, nor did I want them to think I was a flirt or was seeking after their attention. Plus, I did not know who was married and who wasn't, and I did not want any negative situations occurring.

Working at the Exchange opened up many opportunities to meet new people, including coworkers and customers. And on occasion, many interesting things would happen. On one particular day, an incident occurred that I will never forget. I was standing at the end of the cash register, and a man walked by me holding balloons, flowers, and candy. Normally, someone with something to celebrate would look bubbly, alive, and filled with happiness. But, not that man. He looked very stiff and stoic. Then, I heard one of my coworkers call the man's name. She recognized him, but a startled look crossed his face and his fingers loosened the grasp he had on the balloons. Slowly, the balloons began to float upward. To alleviate their escape, I quickly reached up and grabbed them, while saying, "Oh, no. You don't want to lose these!" As I handed the balloons back to the man, the startled look was still plastered on his face. He went on to complete his purchase and left to continue his day.

The next evening, I was driving to a friend's house, and I turned into the cul-de-sac where she lived. I drove past a house that had yellow caution tape displayed across it, and military police cars were parked everywhere. I wondered what had transpired, and I knew it was serious because of the number of officers on the scene. When I arrived to my friend's house, she filled me in, saying a murder had been committed. Later that evening, I saw the story on the news and learned a woman had been murdered. When I went to work the next day, the coworker, who had called out the man's name, told me it was the wife of that man (who had purchased the balloons, candy, and flowers) who had been murdered, and her husband was the one who had committed the crime.

I didn't know what to make of that. We had just seen him in the store the day before. The first thought that went through my mind was *I wish I could have said something to him that would have impacted the course of events.* You never know what people are dealing with, and one word could cause a positive change in someone's world.

On a more positive note, I began to see the young man, who I had first seen on the beach and then at church, walking through the Exchange. After walking about the store, he would bring his purchases through my checkout line. I thought it was very interesting, but at first I refrained from sharing my thoughts aloud. Eventually though, I asked when he would be coming back to church because I had not seen him in a few Sundays. He simply replied he did not know when he would return. Also, to ensure he was on base legally and not just a weird stalker, I asked to see his military I.D., which he did produce. That put my mind at ease. Later, I realized he must have been working the swing shift, which was the shift directly after mine. That explained why he would shop during my shift.

As the days and weeks went by, we continued our light banter whenever he was in the Exchange. Sometimes, instead of being at the cash register, I would restock shelves. As I would move about the store, he would walk with me and assist me with replacing items on shelves and helping me with whatever I was doing. A friendship was blossoming between us. After that went on for a while, I finally decided I needed to know his name, so I formally introduced myself as LaMonica, and he introduced himself as Antwon.

On one particular day, I decided to take the conversation to a more personal level by asking Antwon if he had any children. He told me he had a daughter and promptly pulled out a picture of her. I responded by telling him I was the proud mother of two sons who were fifteen and sixteen years of age and that they would beat him up if he got out of line. I laughed as I made my comment, to let him know I was joking. Then, catching him off guard, I asked, "Do you want to take me out?" In a bit of shock, Antwon looked at me and paused. The pause lasted so long that I jumped in and offered my own response, saying, "You don't have to." I felt awkward as the moment seemed as though it was moving in slow motion. Finally, after giving my question some thought, he said, "Sure."

That night, Antwon came to my apartment to pick me up for our date. Knowing C was probably watching me from his apartment, as Antwon and I walked to his car, I slowly took his hand into mine, to send a clear message to C that we were done.

Antwon and I went to see a movie at the drive-in theater. As I continued to size him up, something I had begun to do at the Exchange, I noticed he drove a nice car. And, the fact he had a daughter and kept her picture with him made me think he was a good father to her and therefore would be a good father to my sons and offer stability in my life. Those were the thoughts that had begun to form during the days we had spent time together as I worked.

After enjoying our time at the movies, we went back to my apartment and engaged in a bit more intimacy by exploring each other's bodies. Where our actions led caused a shock to my system....

A few months later, I went to the doctor and learned I was with child once again. The first thought that jumped into my mind was, *I got pregnant on the first night we were together*, and the first thought that entered my heart was, *Now, I will have three children with three different fathers.* That realization left a sinking feeling in the pit of my stomach. But, what could I do? I was the one who had created my own conditions. I could not point the finger at anyone else. The situation I then found myself in was a result of the choices I had made. My loneliness, my need and desire for love and affection, and my impulsiveness had all led me to my current situation. Therefore, I was the one who had to cope with the outcome. That truth rang over and over in my mind.

A few Sundays later, at the drive-in movie theater, I approached the pastor's wife and told her my news. With a straight face, she looked directly at me and asked, "What are you going to do?" I shared with her what I had already decided- that I would take responsibility for my actions by raising my children- alone if I had to. Later, I told Antwon about my conversation with the first lady. In response, he shared his own thoughts: "I will be there to take care of my baby. Wherever I go, you are going," he said, meaning if he was deployed from his military post, I would go with him wherever he may be required to go. I was pleasantly surprised to hear his words.

As time moved forward, I learned the state of our relationship was not as I had assumed when a friend of mine divulged she had seen Antwon at the mall with another girl with whom he was walking and holding hands. There I was at home with a growing belly and off he was keeping company with another woman. What nerve! From my perspective, he and I were in a committed relationship, but for him (based on the news I had received), he was not.

So, of course, I would not be who I am if I had just let the information roll by without addressing it with him directly. When I broached the subject with him, he gave me a lame excuse for why he was walking hand in hand with another woman. He said, "She is so beautiful and did not want men trying to talk to her, so I was holding her hand to keep the men away." I knew he was not being honest with me, so my anger rose. In my outrage, I broke one of his CD's and threw a fork at him as he was walking down the stairs from my apartment, when I told him to leave.

A couple of days later, I saw Antwon driving alongside of me with his lady friend, the same one he had been seen with at the mall. Gesturing from my car, I told him to drop her off and to meet me at my friend's house. He complied with my request and met me there a bit later. From his actions, I understood he was still attempting to prove his point to me that I was the only one he was concerned about. To take his efforts a step further, while we were visiting my friend's home, we decided to sneak away for a private moment in the bathroom. At two to three months pregnant, I was ecstatic about what I believed he was expressing to me. I interpreted his actions of pulling his car over and taking the girl home to mean he wanted us to move forward with our relationship. I was thrilled, causing my outlook about our relationship to shift 180°. Because I was in total agreement about us moving forward, I began planning our wedding.

A few days later, Antwon came over to visit, and we had a long talk about our relationship. He committed to me on that day, and I committed to him. His actions told me I was not completely disillusioned about how he felt about me, but I still did not understand why he would be out with someone else. However, I was determined to move forward.

One Sunday at church, Antwon and I walked up to the pastor's wife. After making idle chitchat, I told her I was getting married. Without responding directly to me, she shifted her focus to Antwon and asked him it that were true. He said, "No, I did not ask her to marry me." Hearing his words caused me to go immediately into emotional distress. I was very embarrassed, and I felt humiliated in front of the pastor's wife. I really did not know what to do, but one thing I was certain about was being done with him and our so-called relationship.

Later that evening, I was still very upset, but Antwon was right by my side on the floor, sitting with his legs crossed. Trying to calm me down and to smooth over what had occurred earlier at church, he explained, "I said that because I had not asked you to marry me yet. I wanted to do it the right way. I don't have a ring yet." Even though he appeared to be sincere, I did not believe anything he was telling me. I believed he was only saying the words to placate me. By the end of the night, he had proposed, and I responded, "We will see."

After he left, I continued sitting on the floor by the floor heater (my favorite spot), crying uncontrollably. Looking back, my actions were reminiscent of the many times I had sat inside my closet screaming and crying as a result of the emptiness that filled me to my core. During my episodes, I would ask God why I was alone without family and without a special person in my life to provide love and care for me and for my sons. Compounding my anxiety, I would also pray and cry out because I would have dreams about the Rapture. Deep down, I had an awareness that God was doing something in my life while at the same time feeling as though He did not hear me. I felt dead inside, and the loneliness was torturing me. It was as though God was not hearing my cry for help.

A few days later, Antwon and I continued our conversation. My heart was still very hardened against him but because I really wanted to live out the fairytale I had fantasized about for so long, I accepted his words and agreed to marry him. We went looking for a ring the next day.

At one time, before we met, Antwon had proposed to his daughter's mother. However, they obviously possessed two different ideas about their relationship because she refused the proposal. At that point in our relationship, he still had the rings he had purchased for her. After we became engaged, he eventually sold the rings and used the money to purchase my engagement ring.

I was over the top with excitement about the wedding, so the planning re-commenced. We were looking forward to a life that was right in the sight of God. We were fully aware that we had committed sin, and we wanted a fresh start. Plus, we desired to bring our child into a holy union.

Even though informing the pastor's wife about us getting married was what had spurred Antwon into action, I had long since held the idea of marriage in my mind. Once people knew we were an expectant couple, they had begun to plant the seed of marriage into our minds by telling us we should go ahead and get married. Plus, always having dreamt about being married when I was a young girl, it seemed as though my dream would finally come true. Furthermore, I realized if I were to fulfill my dream, after having two children out of wedlock, the wagging tongues of judgment would more than likely cease. Unbeknownst to me, I was living in a fairytale world.

In the midst of preparing for my big day, I received a completely unexpected call from my neighbor's son, Vincent- the one who had babysat my sons while I made a quick grocery run. By that time, we lived even closer in proximity because I had moved to a three-bedroom apartment in their building. Our families had grown even closer in the year and a half time frame that had passed. I had continued to spend time with the mother and the children, teaching one of them to drive.

On that day though, I was not expecting Vincent's call or what he was about to share with me. In a low, shaky voice, he said, "I need to tell you something." I ignored the mysterious tone in his voice and tried to guess what his call was about. "Did you hit my car?" I asked, wondering if Vincent had hit Antwon's very nice Cadillac that he simply adored. Quickly, he said, "No." My heart immediately felt relief. Well, ... until I heard Vincent's confession.

He confession was regarding the night he had babysat my sons. He stated when he changed my baby son's diaper, he had fondled him and put his mouth on my son's penis. I went immediately into shock and began to ask questions, such as, "Why?" and "Why are you telling me this now?" To the latter question, he responded, "I feel guilty, and I needed to get it off me." Hearing me yell and scream in the midst of crying, Antwon who had been sitting on the couch was then standing, wondering who was on the phone and what the person could have possibly been saying to me to incite such a reaction.

I was in a state of bewilderment. I did not know what to do, and the only thing I could think to do was go talk to my pastor, who was the one the congregation turned to for everything. We had absolute trust in him. So, I drove over to the church. It was customary to have an appointment with the pastor rather than just dropping in. However, that was an emergency, and I made haste. Upon my arrival, I was crying hysterically, and the pastor heard my sounds of agony. He came out and immediately ushered me into his office.

I shared with him the account of abuse Vincent has just called and confessed to me. My pastor suggested I not tell anyone about the incident. He assured me there was another way to handle the situation. He said the church would get Vincent the help he needed to deal with his issue, which plain and simple was pedophilia.

After leaving the church, I spoke to a good friend of mine, the pastor's daughter, and told her what had occurred. Surprisingly, Vincent had called her as well to inform her of another confession that was obviously tormenting him. Sometime ago, he had babysat her two-year-old daughter, and on that occasion, the toddler was crying continuously and would not cease. In his frustration with her whimpering, he picked her up and threw her against the couch to make her stop crying. Like me, my friend was appalled to learn his secret and began to carry the same burden of frustration, disappointment, hurt, and lack of trust. Upon learning about the abuse of my son, I immediately became suspicious of everyone, which led to me becoming overprotective of my children. However, Vincent's confession was only the beginning of a nightmare!

To exacerbate the turmoil that was developing in my personal life, I was faced with another situation to deal with. One night, during our engagement, I was asleep on the couch, and Antwon was directly below me on the floor. Like me, he was fast asleep. As we slept, a dream crept upon me, causing me to become unsettled in my spirit. I dreamt Antwon had cheated on me, but with whom he had cheated was not revealed to me in the dream. I awoke with a start and immediately awakened him from his slumber. I shared the dream with him and asked if it were true that he had or was cheating on me.

To my surprise, he confessed. He stated he had slept with the girl he had been with at the mall and in the car. I asked him when it happened, and he stated it happened on the same day that I had seen him in the car with her. I was alarmed by his response. After a bit more conversation, I learned he had engaged in sexual intercourse with her prior to meeting me at my friend's home. To compound matters, he had not only slept with her, but he had not showered before coming to my friend's house and engaging with me during our private moment in the bathroom. I was infuriated by his behavior. I could not believe he had actually committed such an offense against me. The only thing I could think of at that moment was I had a decision to make about my future.

To assist in making my decision, I first needed to voice my concerns and thoughts, so I confided in my pastor's wife. In response to what I shared with her regarding the dream I had and Antwon's confession, she said, "It is good God showed you what is going on, so you won't have reservations about your marriage later." Despite her words of wisdom, I was operating with a made-up mind regarding my engagement and impending marriage. I decided long ago I would one day fulfill my desire of being married, something I had wanted since I was a young girl. Even though I had reservations about marrying Antwon, I was determined to move forward because there was nothing I wanted more than to be married. So, talking with her and receiving advice was a really moot point because I was headed toward the wedding aisle.

Soon, February 5, 2000 -the big day- arrived! At eight months pregnant, I walked down the aisle- approximately a month and a half before I was due to deliver our child on March 20th. It was a day I had looked forward to with great anticipation.

Unfortunately, the groom was not having the same experience of excitement. Prior to the wedding day, Antwon had invited several of his friends to be included in our wedding, but they did not accept his invitation because they did not share in his happiness. To compound matters, Antwon's friends would speak negatively about me, desiring to change his mind about marrying me. Demonstrating his passivity, he would not say a word in my defense. When I addressed the issue, all he would say to them was, "You should hang up the phone the next time you want to talk about someone." I found his response irritating and hurtful because from my viewpoint, he was allowing his so-called friends to disrespect his soon-to-be wife and mother of his unborn child. To compound matters, his parents did not share in his joy either. In retrospect, that must have been really hard for him to deal with, but for me, all I cared about was getting and being married.

I was so caught up in my world of fantasy that I even tuned out the voice of the pastor when I was in counseling sessions listening to the do's and don'ts of marriage. The words reached my head and went into one ear and out the other. The only thing I heard was my own voice and the desires that resided within me.

On the day of the wedding, as I was having my hair styled, my pastor's wife asked me if I was sure I wanted to get married. Without hesitation, I said, "Yeah!" I was determined to move forward. I had awaited that day for a very long time, and I would not be talked out of moving forward with my plans.

At the wedding, with the support of my family, my grandfather walked me down the aisle. I smiled as I allowed my excitement to fill me and overflow. My cup was truly filled with excitement from all of the festivities. My godmother, who was a real mother to me, and Sandra, a good friend, along with some of the church members really went all out because they wanted my day to be special. They rallied around me to make sure everything was set the way I desired them to be. Someone baked and decorated the wedding cake; another person made our dresses; and my godmother created the invitations. To top things off, my best friend flew in from California to be with me. Everyone pitched in and did their part, and they truly made my day spectacular.

In retrospect, I know Antwon did not feel exactly the same way because his family refused to come and support him. The only one who was in attendance was his aunt. Unfortunately for me, the excited that had surrounded me quickly dissipated once the ceremony and reception were over. On the night of the wedding, nothing went as planned. Instead of joy overflowing, tears of realization flooded from my eyes, for I knew I had just made the biggest mistake of my life not even realizing why. Later I would learn that I would cry many tears. Antwon, in his naiveté, asked me why I was crying. I could not bring myself to tell him the truth. Instead, I told him I had discomfort in my stomach.

On March 20, 2000, at nearly twenty-three years of age, I gave birth to my third bundle of joy, my first baby girl whom I named Tyonna Renee Davis. She weighed in at six pounds, being so small she could fit inside a diaper bag. Having and holding her brought me so much happiness, and once again, my cup of joy was running over. Actually, it had been overflowing from the moment I learned I was having a baby girl, which was when I selected her name. Each day, I sat and held her, looking down into her very large eyes, which made her look like an alien baby. But, she was MY alien baby. I could not love her any more if she were any different.

Once my daughter and I were released from the hospital, I had a great deal of support awaiting me at home. Prior to going to the hospital to deliver, my mother had arrived a few days earlier from California, so she could be with my sons while my husband and I went to the hospital. Once I had returned home and settled in with my baby girl, I began to prepare for my mother-in-law's arrival.

Because I had never met her, I wanted to make a good first impression. She was flying into town from Georgia for the visit, and my daughter and I would be meeting her at the same time. The first thing Antwon and I had to figure out was where his mother was going to sleep. In our three-bedroom, Antwon and I had our room, our two sons had their room, and the baby had her room, which was also being used as a place to store unused items. My mother was sleeping in the boys' room on their bunkbeds, so the only room for my mother-in-law to sleep in was the baby's room. That meant I had some cleaning to do.

When my mother saw the effort I was putting in to make my mother-in-law comfortable, she went off on one of her tirades. Apparently, she was jealous because she thought I was going over the top for my husband's mother, and from her perspective, I had not done the same for her. I told her what I thought about her comments, but I kept right on doing what needed to be done.

Although I was really looking forward to meeting my mother-in-law in person, my own mother was ruining the anticipation for me. It seemed as though every time we would get into a spat, she would make a contrary statement, such as, "I can't wait for her to see how such a disrespectful little girl you are!" Her comments infuriated me, and I was determined to prove her wrong. While hearing her taunts, I made up my mind that I would not be a hypocrite. Instead, I would remain the same even if I did not fully know who I was at that time in my life. In retrospect, I realize I was vulnerable and unsure of myself, as I was coming into my own.

Also, in retrospect, I now realize the enemy was setting me up to sabotage myself. By trying to prove my mother wrong, I was only falling into the enemy's plan of defeat for my life. Part of the enemy's plan was to lead me into longing for my pastor's approval and trusting him and his wife explicitly because of who they stated themselves to be- people of God, a man and woman of the cloth. Trusting them came with seeking their opinion on nearly every aspect of my life. In my mind, who better to trust than those who represent the King? Little did I know what the enemy had planned for me because I had opened the door of my life to them.

Overall, my mother stayed with us for about a month. Antwon's mother only stayed throughout the weekend, which turned out to be enough time for her to be in our home.

Other than the mothers being there to help out, my friends from our church group Young Excited Adults with Hope (Y.E.A.H.), for ages eighteen to twenty-eight, would stop by to visit as well. We had really become a close-knit group from all the time we had spent together doing outreach, praying, and fellow-shipping. Our ministry was the livelihood of the church, and once I was married, the pastor allowed me to be over the prayer group. I had developed into a strong prayer warrior, who would at times prophecy as I prayed as the Spirit of the Lord overshadowed me.

When my friends from Y.E.A.H. would visit, they would bring food and sit, laugh, and joke with us. One of the jokes was about my baby girl: "She's going to be cute one day!" I laughed along with everyone else. I knew Tyonna wasn't the cutest baby, but I knew she would grow into her cuteness, and we all loved her just the same.

During my mother-in-law's visit, I thought it would be the perfect time to have Tyonna's baby dedication, so both of our mothers could attend. However, my mother was diametrically opposed to the idea. She went on and on about how I should not go outside so soon after giving birth, and I agreed with her, but I also believed I could make an exception while Antwon's mother was in town. I decided to get a second opinion from my pastor. Why did I say that aloud? That was all that was needed to send my mother over the edge and into one of her rants. She actually became belligerent and began to talk about me to my mother-in-law who apparently took her side. I drew that conclusion by the way she treated me afterward. We really did not have a relationship to begin with, and I knew she thought Antwon and I had married far too soon, but I was hoping to begin developing one while she was there. That was a hope that went unrealized, and I do not believe she gave me a fair chance to get to know the person I was and the wife I would be to her son.

In my mother's outburst, she accused me of being controlling-amongst other things. She also mentioned how dirty the baby's room was as if though Antwon and I did not make a regular practice of cleaning our home. She said that in front of my mother-in-law in another attempt to embarrass me. Then, my mother was so enraged that she grabbed my face and threatened to knock me out. When I could no longer stand hearing her voice, I proceeded to leave the house and took my tears and my husband with me, telling him, "Come on. Let's go!" Hearing my command, my mother took that opportunity to tell Antwon's mother, "See! She controls him, too!"

While I was out, I went to my godmother's house to cool off and get a bit of advice about the situation with my mother, who I felt was still trying to control my life, not only while she was in town but from California as well. Once I had calmed down enough to hear the voice of reason, my godmother told me, "You are grown, married with children, and you live in your own home and pay your own bills. Be respectful to your mother, but let her know you can and will make your own decisions." When I spoke to my pastor, he gave me the same advice. So, I puffed up my chest and dried my tears. When I returned home, I shared my perspective with my mother. Why, oh why did I do that? The situation only grew worse. It was as though I was fighting a never-ending battle with my mother. In her eyes, I was always a child to her and things had to go her way and that was that.

Despite the concerns my mother had voiced, my daughter's dedication took place on the next Sunday afternoon, at the end of the regular Sunday service. Although I had agreed with her regarding the wisdom of staying indoors six to eight weeks after giving birth as I had done after the birth of both my sons, I felt it was necessary to make an exception that time to take advantage of the fact both my daughter's grandmothers were present and could therefore both attend the dedication service.

After the blow up with my mother, I had spoken to my pastor to solicit his opinion regarding having the dedication the following Sunday. Because he agreed it would be a good idea, we moved forward with the plan. The dedication was short and sweet, and I was so happy that I had decided to go ahead with my plan. At that time, my daughter was only two to three weeks old, which means I had stayed indoors for less than a month. After having the dedication, I resumed my regular church attendance from that point forward, suspending the six-to-eight week at-home-stay period indefinitely. The following Monday, my mother-in-law returned home, and my mother remained in my home a few days longer, which caused the tension level to remain high.

All the while our mothers were in our midst and giving me stress, another stressful situation was brewing. From the time Antwon and I had begun dating, I noticed he would constantly receive phone calls from his ex-fiancé. Their constant communication was foreign to me and appeared unnecessary. I did not believe they needed to communicate about their daughter as much as they were communicating and did not understand what else they would need to talk about. Although the calls frustrated me, I did not feel as though I had a right to share my perspective with Antwon because we were only dating, so I said nothing. I was even more disturbed when I found out he had spoken to her on the day of our wedding to inform her he was getting married. I learned later that his ex was also pregnant with her second child, and upon hearing his news of our marriage, she became distraught and went into labor.

Then, a few days after our daughter was born, she called him, and the first thing out of his mouth was, "She had the baby." I was instantly frustrated, wondering why he felt the need to keep her informed about our business.

My perspective on how much they were communicating quickly changed once we were married. So, when the opportunity presented itself to share my outlook about his constant contact with his daughter's mother, that's exactly what I did. I told him his ex-fiancé needed to stop calling so much, and I questioned him about keeping her informed about what was going on in our life. I did not understand the purpose, and I wanted it to cease. He just looked at me with a dumfounded look and remained quiet... as usual.

After being married a couple of months, the child support my husband was paying to his ex was taking a toll on our finances and standard of living. Due to his rank in the military, he was not bringing in much money, and I had become a stay-at-home mother, after leaving my place of employment. He was paying

$400 a month in child support, but I requested he cut the amount in half because we really did not have the finances to be able to spend $400 a month for his daughter. He agreed, and the $200 he kept was a benefit to us. Thankfully, our expenses were not too high because we did live rent free in military housing and were only responsible for paying for our cell phones, cable, car note and car insurance each month. I would contribute to the household income by taking odd jobs here and there, such as babysitting and completing do-it-yourself projects. Also, both of my sons' fathers were paying child support. So, we had a little cushion to help meet our needs.

A few months into the marriage, my husband received his first notice of deployment. The unexpected notice sent a wave of sadness over me. The women in my life (those on the base, my godmother, and the women at church) rallied around me and provided a support system. Despite my husband being gone, I truly felt as though I had made it in my life by being a military wife, which had also been a long-time desire. However, in the midst of having all my dreams fulfilled, I did not realize my husband and I were not effectively communicating. I was blinded by my lifestyle, and the days were passing us by.

One night, I had a dream I will never forget. In the dream, my husband and I were on an airplane, flying to an unknown destination. When the airplane landed, it began taxing through a graveyard. From my seat, as I looked through the window, I saw tombstones everywhere. When I awoke, I felt a creepy sensation all over me. I had always been terrified of anything that had to do with death. The same was true for my mother; the fear of death was a generational curse upon my family. It was so strong that even for me to pass by a cemetery or see someone dead, I would feel as though I was going to die. Having that dream left an earie feeling in my spirit.

Reflections

Read the following questions, reflect upon your own life, and use this space as a private place to write.

Question 1- Do you have a weakness? If so, what is it, and why is it a weak area in your life?

_____

_____

Question 2- How do or did you cope with your weakness?

_____

_____

Question 3- Do you have someone whom you can trust to talk to? Who is that person?

_____

_____

Question 4- Have you confessed your weakness to anyone?

_____

_____

Question 5- How did he/she respond to you?

_____

_____

2

Living in Reality

A few days later though, I understood the message of the dream. My husband received a call from a family member, saying his grandmother, who had been on hospice, had passed away. So, when the time for the funeral approached, Antwon, I, and our daughter flew to Georgia. That must be where we were headed in the dream and why we were on an airplane. For the trip, we would be leaving our sons in the care of my mother who was required to fly in from California. Our departure and her arrival would be on the same day, so we coordinated our flight schedules. Upon my mother's arrival to the airport from California, we would be flying out to Georgia. After her plane arrived, we met her and gave her the keys to our home and the keys to the Cadillac. As she made her way to the base, we made our way to our departure terminal.

Upon landing in Georgia, we took the long drive to Antwon's mother's house. I was overflowing with excitement to meet my husband's family because I had not had an opportunity to meet them before, as none of them attended our wedding. However, I was also filled with an uneasy feeling about seeing his mother due to what had transpired the first time we met. After we arrived and had greeted everyone who was present, we settled into his teenage sister's room, which was where we would be sleeping during our stay there.

Later that day, Antwon sent his sister over to his daughter's house to make arrangements for her to be picked up later. He was anxious to see her, and I was looking forward to meeting her for the first time. However, I was not interested in any drama that could possibly ensue with her mother Dawn. To ward off any problems before they could arise, I had already given Antwon a pep talk about his interactions with her prior to leaving home. I informed him that I did not want to deal with her constant phone calls during the time we were in town or anything else that could possibly occur.

The next day, the plan was to assist with his grandmother's funeral arrangements. We made our way to the funeral home, and just being there terrified me. At one point, I needed to go to the restroom. A voice in my head warned me to not look to my left, but having a hard head, I looked anyway. When I did, my fear level rose exponentially because I was then confronted with a row of caskets. At that moment, I felt as though I would die and someone would put me in one of the caskets. In an attempt to assuage my fear, I called my mother and told her what I was experiencing. She said, "You did not like that, huh?" I agreed, saying I definitely did not.

Later, it was time to go to the burial site to choose a plot. Then, after all the business for the funeral had been taken care of, we made our way to the mall because the next day the family would be wearing white, and I did not have any white attire. So, Antwon and I along with our daughter, his younger brother and his best friend's younger brother (both were teenagers) went to the mall to shop. I was excited to go to the mall and to see all the surroundings of the city because I had never been there before. Meanwhile, Antwon's daughter had been picked up by his sister and taken to his mother's house, so we could see her upon our return.

While we were walking around the mall with the baby, the teenage boys ran up to us to take our baby daughter with them as they walked about the mall. I told them, "Don't try to get girls with our baby." I laughed as I handed her over. Having a moment of freedom from any child responsibilities, Antwon and I walked into a department store. Antwon looked up and saw his daughter's mother. He said, "There's Dawn." I responded, "So!" and continued going in the opposite direction. At that moment, he was hugging me from behind, and I directed him through the racks of clothes. Do you know Dawn followed us with her baby through the clothes?

After she approached us, we introduced ourselves, and Antwon greeted her. After speaking to her, he made a face at her by blowing air into his cheeks, signaling he could see she had gained weight. Right at that moment, the boys brought our daughter back. They had not taken her to help them catch girls; they had taken her to see Dawn. I guess she had wanted to see our daughter. Dawn also had a baby girl, so Antwon introduced the two babies to each other, saying, "Meet your sister."

I immediately became unraveled. I did not understand why he would say that. To me, he was giving Dawn false hope about a future relationship between the two of them. Secondly, the babies were not related. But, instead of going off and making a scene, I decided it would be best to simply walk away, so that's what I did. Did my husband follow me? Ummm, noooo. He stayed there and continued talking as if though all was well. Finally, I called his name. He answered, "Yes?" I replied, "Come on..."

He came, and I promptly went off on him, asking why he would say what he said when there is no relation between the babies. My anger in turn incited anger within him. Seeing we were getting nowhere with our conversation, I said I was going to leave and go back to his mother's home, although I had no idea how I would get there. In his anger, he bumped into our daughter's stroller, causing her to bump her head on the inside of the stroller. He didn't rub her head or apologize. I did not appreciate his actions at all. In the midst of all of that, Dawn appeared and looked over at us. I did not want her to know we were fighting, so I put on a brave face.

Soon after, I went outside the mall, so I could figure out how to get back to his mother's house, in a city I had never been in and did not know my way around. A bit later, Antwon came looking for me. He found me at a phone booth, as I was preparing to call a taxi. His mother came to the mall to pick all of us up, so the taxi ride was no longer required.

On the ride back to her house, Antwon told his mother what had transpired regarding Dawn. She immediately took on his perspective, saying the babies are family, and it's better to keep people out of your business. I did not see her point, and as I looked around to see who agreed with me, everyone was quiet.

As expected yet undesired, Dawn called Antwon not too long after we had returned to his mother's house. He was on the phone with her for a long time. When he finished, I asked him what she wanted. Essentially, she wanted to have a one-on-one face-to-face meeting with Antwon and told him, "Your wife can come too if she wants to." I looked at him as though Dawn must have been crazy to even suggest I needed permission to take part in the meeting. I told him, "As your wife, I *am* coming!"

After the funeral the next day, we went over to Dawn's house for the "meeting." Her primary concern seemed to be when he would be coming back to visit their daughter. Because he was still on active duty in the military, he did not have an answer to her question. Of course, his non-answer did not sit well with her, which seemed to upset her because she wasn't getting her way with him. From my perspective, she could have asked that question over the phone instead of calling a face-to-face meeting.

After the funeral, I had an opportunity to meet my husband's family, which was nice. Then, before I knew it, after being there a total of three days, our trip came to an end.

During the ride to the airport, Antwon, his brother, his mother, his friend, and I were all in the car. As we rode, everyone was making small talk, but his friend continuously brought up Antwon and Dawn's past relationship. He shared many details, even how they would frequent hotels together. He was very annoying, and although everyone kept telling him to shut up, he continued running his mouth. To me, it was as though he was rubbing the closeness of their relationship in my face by making a point about how they would do everything together. I felt humiliated. But, in the midst of everything Antwon's friend shared, I learned their relationship was deeper than I had previously thought. And, that realization was painful. Actually, the pain I felt was excruciating. I also learned everyone liked Dawn, which explained why I received so much hostility from the family.

As time progressed, I would discover there was definitely a soul tie between Antwon and Dawn that had not been uprooted, which would explain the constant communication, etc. Once we were back home in Jersey, unfortunately our marriage continued on its downward spiral.

The next March, when our baby girl was turning a year old, my mother and younger brother came to visit us and to celebrate my younger brother's and my daughter's birthdays. He was turning six, and she was turning one. Their birthdays are a week apart. We all had a really good time at the huge block party we threw. There was a huge bounce house, good music, and good food. It was well attended by our neighbors and a lot of people from the church, and everyone was in a festive mood.

Shortly after Antwon's deployment ended, his dedicated time in the service of four years of active duty had come to an end as well. However, he had also enlisted for four years as a reservist, which would directly follow his four years of active duty. He had to decide if he would enlist for another term or if he would walk away from the life of a service man. Ultimately, against my desires of continuing on with our current lifestyle, he stated he had completed his designated time and believed God was saying his time was up and that he could move forward with his original plan of only serving his country for four years and returning to Georgia afterward. I told him God had changed his plan, and I personally had no desire to move to Georgia away from our church. Instead, we moved locally into a three-bedroom house because Antwon did not continue on with his service, requiring us to move from military housing.

Instead, he took on a civilian job that would bring in more income than he was earning in the military. On the surface, that sounded good, but in reality, it was not because he failed to factor in the two-hour drive each way and the cost of gas. We shifted from only paying four bills to paying rent, utilities, cable, and car note. With the increased expenses, we could no longer afford car insurance. Not only was our financial status impacted, our time with each other was cut short. Antwon would leave home each day at 4am and did not return until 8pm due to his extended commute. I was very frustrated with our change in circumstances, and I missed him dearly. I would call him all day, and I am certain my constant calls disturbed his boss, but that was the least of my concerns.

One day, while Antwon was at work, his daughter's mother made continuous calls to our house phone. I answered her each time and let her know Antwon was not available, but on the fourth call, I asked if something was wrong. She said everything was okay, but she needed to talk to Antwon. I told her I would let him know to call her. I called him on the cell phone while he was driving home from work. He said he would call her to find out what she wanted. When he arrived home that evening, I asked him what she had wanted. At first, he acted as though it was no big deal, but I kept pressing him to be truthful with me. So finally, he stated not too long ago he had asked his ex why they had broken up. Immediately, I was concerned about what I was hearing. I didn't understand why he would ask that question at that point in our lives. There we were married and had been over a year and a few months. So, I asked him why he wanted to know the reason for their break up now. He did not answer me with words. Instead, he gave me a dumbfounded look. In my mind and heart, I felt as though there was something going on between the two of them, which was leading her to consistently call our home. In the midst of the conversation, he also confessed she had dedicated Aaliyah's song "I Miss You" to him, and in turn, he had dedicated "Cry Me a River" by Justin Timberlake to her. That statement alone spoke volumes to me about what was on his mind.

A few months later, I learned I was pregnant. We were excited to receive the news, but another upset in our life was on the horizon. The house we were renting had been placed on the market to be sold by the owner, and the realtor would show up often with potential buyers, showing them the house. That was not only disappointing but disruptive as well. But, as usual, life had to move on, and we had to prepare to move again.

Meanwhile, I was a young mother of three who was preparing to deliver another child in the coming months. I was accustomed to being healthy and bouncing back after giving birth. So, I engaged in physical activities as I normally would. One day while attending a church picnic, I was playing Double Dutch with the girls, and I began bleeding. At four months pregnant, I was quite surprised and concerned, so I immediately went to the emergency room at the military hospital as we still had our military benefits. The doctor placed me on bed rest and advised me to see my primary care doctor as soon as possible.

Following his advice, I followed up by seeing my primary doctor. To my utter surprise, I found him to be very rude when he stated, "You can just get off bedrest because if the baby is going to die, it will die anyway." I was put off by the callousness of my doctor and his blunt disposition. I shared his comments with the nurse who was just as appalled as I was at the doctor's words. To assuage my fears, she immediately performed an ultrasound, reporting my baby was healthy. She advised me to continue my regular activities but to be careful while doing so. Ending our visit, she said, "We will see you in December around your due date." I left with peace of mind.

Afterward, the roller coaster ride that came next was both unwanted and tiresome. Our home was sold, so the anticipated move had finally come. Looking for a place that was affordable was not easy, but thankfully we had friends in our corner who had our best interest in mind. One of them recommended a guy they knew who had come to our church who owned several apartment buildings. We knew who they were referring to and decided to give him a call to see if he had any vacancies. After getting in contact with him, we learned he had a two-bedroom townhouse for rent. Being desperate, we had to overlook the condition of the building, which was in great need of repair, and its location, which was in the woods down the road from my friend Michelle. We were required to submit first and last month's rent. We did as we were asked, and we moved in. It was not the best place to live, but it met our needs and would suffice for the five of us at that point.

After dealing with the increase in expenses and the recent move, bitterness towards Antwon and our situation really began to kick in. I did not know how much more I was willing to deal with. From my perspective, if he had just stayed in the military, life would have continued as normal, and we would not be going through the changes that were plaguing us and our young family.

It did not take long for trouble to rear its ugly head again- two months to be exact. Sadly, we learned the property owner was losing his property, which meant we were losing our home. We tried contacting him by phone, but he refused to answer or return our calls. We shared our concerns with our neighbors who thought we were crazy and just lying. I suggested they refrain from continuing to pay rent, but they ignored my advice and paid anyway- only to lose their money because we all had to move out a few months later.

In the midst of dealing with our living conditions, another problem brewed. One day, as Antwon was driving across the bridge that would allow him to exit the island, the tires of the van hit black ice, sending the minivan into a tailspin. It hit a log barrier and was suspended in air, hanging off the bridge. If Antwon had been driving faster than the five miles an hour he was going, he would have gone completely over the edge. Praise God, he made it through the incident safely. Unfortunately, we did not have car insurance, so we were unable to get the vehicle repaired and had to drive around in the beat-up van.

Knowing we would soon be moving from the townhome, we decided it would be best to begin looking for suitable accommodations. One morning, as Antwon was driving to work, we were conversing via telephone and decided that particular day would be a good day to begin searching for a new home. The thought occurred to us that we could look for accommodations off the island although neither of us had ever lived off the island before and had some concerns about doing so.

The plan was for the children and me to drive to Antwon's job to meet him when he got off work, and from there, we would visit available rentals. As I prepared to leave home and embark upon the two-hour drive, I noticed an extreme amount of moisture was continuing to exit from my body, which had begun earlier that morning. Although it was odd to have leakage at twenty-three weeks pregnant, I wasn't too concerned because the fluid wasn't bloody. If it had been, I would have had more cause for concern. Being mindful, I decided to keep my eyes on the leakage just in case it became increasingly heavier.

Traveling in the van, the children and I arrived at Antwon's job only to find we were met with darkness. So, instead of attempting to look for rentals, I suggested we go to the Naval commissary to purchase groceries. Antwon followed behind us in the Cadillac. While at the store, I felt a sudden urge to go to the restroom. While inside, I began cramping and felt the need to relieve myself, but I dared not do more than urinate in the public bathroom, deciding to wait until I returned home to fully relieve myself.

After the grocery shopping had been completed, we decided to begin the two-hour journey back home, so we jumped on the freeway. However, as we were driving, another idea came to my mind. There was a restaurant we loved called Philly's Best. We were in the area, so I signaled to Antwon to pull alongside me. He did, and I told him my idea. He agreed, so we stopped driving north and pulled off the freeway. While we were sitting at the light to get on the southbound side of the freeway to head in the direction of the restaurant, right at that moment, a sharp cramp went through my stomach, and I screamed out in pain. One of my sons, who was about three or four at the time, must have thought I was joking around, so he began laughing. I tried to signal to Antwon by waving for him to come, but he did not see me. The only thing I had the strength to do amidst all the pain I was experiencing was to make a right turn and pull into the nearest parking lot off the road. Antwon followed me, but he did not get out of the car. I guess he thought I needed to take care of something in the car, so he sat and waited in his car, which was behind me.

After what felt like an eternity, he eventually pulled up next to me to see what was taking me so long to proceed to the freeway. The pain was mounting, and I continued to signal him. It took him a while to get out and come over to me. I was yelling, trying to get him to understand that I was having excruciating pain in my stomach. I felt as though I needed to push because the baby was bearing down in my uterus. I told Antwon to call the police or the paramedic. Finally, he began to understand my need for medical attention. But, in his regular nonchalant manner, he began to walk around to look for help. Finally, he found a bystander who obviously called the paramedics.

I was in so much agony that I was only vaguely aware of what happened next. The next thing I recall was the paramedics being there, yelling for me not to move, which I was continuing to do in an effort to alleviate the amount of pain I was experiencing. I was transported to the hospital, where I learned I had gone into premature labor. The leakage I had been experiencing all day was due to my water bag being torn. Thankfully, it was not completely ruptured. I was given meds to stop the labor from increasing to the point of delivery.

At some point, Antwon called our pastor, and one of the associate pastors and his wife drove over to pick up one of our vehicles and our three children and transported them back to the island. Meanwhile, a team of doctors explained our baby was not going to survive, and they suggested I consent to being induced, so I could deliver my baby that day. After consulting with our pastor, we decided to leave the pregnancy and the state of the baby in God's hands. We would allow His will to be done and go through the pregnancy rather than take matters into our own hands by following the advice of the team of doctors. If our baby were going to die, we were determined to not assist in the process but would allow it to occur naturally.

We communicated our wishes to the doctors, telling them we did not desire for me to be induced and then requested my release. I was sent home with strict instructions to be on bed rest and with antibiotics in the event an infection set in. At that point, my water bag had completely ruptured; however, I did not go into labor.

When I was safely back home, I made myself comfortable downstairs. I only went upstairs to use the restroom. To assist in keeping me still as the doctor had strongly suggested, many of our fellow congregants visited, bringing meals and assisting with housework. I was very grateful for their assistance. Then, about a week later, I had a dream that I had given birth to a son. He was fully dressed in an outfit, which was complete with shoes. Someone laid him on my chest, and as I looked at him, I noticed he did not move.

Having grown tired of lying on the couch day after day, I decided to get up and go into the kitchen to wash the dishes. A strong cramp ran through my abdomen, and without hesitation, I sat down. I called my regular doctor, and she instructed me to go to the hospital immediately. Upon my arrival, I was diagnosed with a fever. After having my blood drawn, I was told my white blood count was high because my body was attempting to reject my baby because it considered him to be a foreign object.

As time went on, I grew increasingly worse so much that both my life and the baby's life were in danger. My pastor and his wife came to hospital to visit me. Seeing the life-threatening condition I was in, she gave me a bit of advice: "You have other children to worry about." Then, she uttered a word of prayer, praying it would not be a long delivery. The instance she stopped praying, I went into labor, and my son was born. Unfortunately, he only lived for one minute. And because he had taken a breath, my husband and I were able to be issued birth and death certificates.

After contacting the funeral home and waiting for their arrival, others arrived and took pictures. My pastor arrived and lifted my baby in his hand as he marveled at God's creation. My son weighed only one pound but was fully formed despite being born prematurely. Amongst the visitors were others who had experienced the same situation. Meanwhile, I was in a state of shock and displayed no emotions. Well actually, I was filled with a sense of dread. I could not understand why God would take our baby from us. I understood we had previously lived a life of sin, but our son was conceived within the covenant of holy matrimony. I felt as though we were being punished. So, I questioned God further. I asked, "Why did this happen to us while we are still serving you?" I was truly perplexed. Then, I was reminded of the scripture regarding the blind man. Someone had asked if he had sinned or if it was his parents who had sinned that led to him being blind. It was revealed that no one had sinned, and the man's blind state was all for the glory of the Lord. Recalling the parable led me to believe the death of my son would in some way bring glory to the Father, but I did not understand how.

It was not until the next morning when I saw the baby bed empty, after the funeral home had taken my baby, that my emotions came flooding through. I wept while Antwon was asleep. Then, after leaving the hospital and passing by the funeral home, I thought, *I have a baby*. And, the tears began to flow again-uncontrollably.

Later that night, Antwon and I were lying in bed talking. I was sharing with him about the men I had slept with in the past, and I began crying. The tears were the Lord's method of cleansing me from my past. I saw balls of fire moving from me. To me, they symbolized the men I had slept with, and the connection to them was departing from me, and I felt a heavy weight lift from me, freeing me.

The next day, Antwon and I had to go to the funeral home to make arrangements for our son's burial. While there, we learned due to size of the baby, he could not be embalmed. Instead, he had to be cremated. Then, we were asked if we wanted to have a memorial service. I did not really think anyone would attend, so I was unsure if we should have one. Some people said they would indeed attend, so we decided to have it, and as promised, people attended. We were given a small urn that held our son's ashes. I was completely devastated about what happened to our son, Joseph T. J. Davis, who was born on August 8, 2001.

Reflections

Read the following questions, reflect upon your own life, and use this space as a private place to write.

Question 1- Have you ever had a dream that came to pass? If so, share it in detail here.

_____

_____

_____

_____

_____

_____

_____

_____

Question 2- How did the dream make you feel?

_____

_____

_____

_____

Question 3- Have you ever loved someone? If so, when and who?

_____

_____

_____

_____

Question 4- How did you communicate with him/her?

_____

_____

_____

_____

Question 5- Did you agree with everything the person said? Why or why not?

_____

_____

_____

_____

3

Taking a Licking and Keeping on Ticking

The death of Joseph, my precious baby boy, did not sit well with me. Although the physicians had thoroughly explained how my placenta had separated from the uterine wall causing Joseph to most likely not survive through a full-term pregnancy, or at the very least, he would make it through the gestation period but end up with special needs. God has an interesting way of providing clarity or insight for me. Usually, my revelations come through dreams.

After asking the Lord repeatedly about Joseph, because my heart was heavy and my belly was empty, I had a dream. In the dream, there was a mother who had several children, and one of them was disabled. I could tell the mother loved all of her children abundantly, but the one with special needs required extra attention and caused her to occasionally be frustrated. In the dream, the Lord was showing me what I would have had to endure with a special needs child, and He knew I would not be able to handle the on-going requirements. After having the dream, I had the revelation that my husband and I should have listened to the wisdom of the doctors because God was speaking to us through them. Being oblivious, we were waiting for God to move and to speak to us. Little did we know that is exactly what He was doing via the physicians. The dream brought clarity to me, giving me peace at last.

After our son's death, Antwon and I received many sympathy cards from family, friends, and church members. The words helped my grief momentarily, but my heart continued to be very heavy as a veil of sadness enveloped me, realizing I would never see him live out his life, running around with his siblings or other children or doing things a well-adjusted little boy would do. However, one of the cards especially touched my heart. Inside was a beautiful poem that demonstrated exactly how I was feeling and also ushered in healing. I have included it below:

As your parents,
we will never sign school papers
or see your name on pictures
that decorate our refrigerator.

The special things kept here
marked your life and death.
Your little footprints
have placed a signature
on our hearts
like no other ever will.

Through it all, I didn't really mourn the death of my son. Of course, I thought about him every day, as my heart overflowed with grief, but I had to focus on my other children and their needs in addition to my husband. There was so much going on in our lives, and there were constantly back-to-back fires to put out. So, I just stuffed my emotions aside and moved on. I had to allow God to heal me. I could not depend on others because no one embraced me or asked how I was doing, nor did I open up and show my emotions to others. I kept everything tucked away.

After our long search for a decent place to live, we were finally able to find a very nice two-bedroom apartment on the third floor of a building in Kant, Jersey, off the island. At that time, we are doing well for ourselves to be able to move that far away. And because we were so far away from our previous residence meant we were also quite far from our church home. To make sure we could continue to worship with other believers, we began looking for a new church home nearby our new residence because driving two hours each way to and from church on Sunday was unrealistic. Although we absolutely loved our pastor, his wife, and the other church members and knew they would always be our family, we did not want to place an undue burden on ourselves or our children. So, I looked in the phone book for local churches, so we could start visiting a few, looking for a new place to call home.

During my search, I located a nearby church and decided to call. The person who answered the phone sounded very welcoming, so we attended their worship service the next Sunday. It was a small church with an African pastor (who had one teenage son) who had an American wife (who had three teenage daughters). We began attending worship services faithfully and became very involved in the ministry there and was on the praise and worship team, as we grew in the Gospel. We even became youth pastors after some time. The freedom and respect we experienced there was vastly different from our former church. That was the beginning of learning who we were in God, understanding we could impact the Kingdom of God with our own voice and God-given authority. I called our former pastor's wife and told her about the spiritual growth in our lives and the elevation we experienced, and she sounded happy, but she did not really embrace what I was sharing with her.

Unbeknownst to me at that time, I was still looking for approval from my former pastors. Unlike them, our new pastors trusted us with the youth and with who we were in God. When the new pastor's wife had trouble dealing with her and her husband's teenage children, who would often be on punishment, they would allow the teens to come to our home with other youth, and we would have gatherings, so we could pour into their lives. At our former church, Antwon and I had desired for them to see us as vessels of honor who could be used for and by God, but our former pastors unfortunately never saw us that way. They wanted to keep us dependent on them for our spiritual needs rather than assisting us in growing spiritually and depending solely on God.

At our new place of worship, we enjoyed the fellowship and even considered the members to be our family, and we still do to this day; however, we did notice instances of racism or discrimination against Americans. For example, I noticed when members would praise dance in the traditional ways Black Americans do, the pastor and the African members would sit quietly. On the other hand, when dancers would praise in the African dance style, the pastor and members would become very animated, demonstrating how much they enjoyed the perfor-mance. Frankly, I did not appreciate the blatant disregard of one dance style versus the other. We tried to display both dance styles, but one was received while the other was not. Meanwhile, while attending our new church home, we kept in touch with our former pastors, calling frequently at first, but over time, our conversations began dwindling.

Settling into our transition, we were thankful that our home life was going well. Our children were doing well with the adjustment, and I had switched the boys into a new preschool and kindergarten class. All was going very well… until one day, I heard Antwon yelling from the bathroom. I ran to see what was the cause for alarm. When I reached the bathroom, Antwon explained to me that the boys had been showering, and when he walked in, they were engaging in inappropriate activity. Hearing the account of what he had witnessed caused me to go immediately into shock, and tears began falling from my eyes. I knew their behavior had something to do with the abuse my youngest son had experienced.

Unbeknownst to me, my older son had experienced abuse as well, but I was unaware at that time. Just recently (while writing this book), a close friend of mine from Jersey reminded me of another friend of ours who at one time at our old church had shared her testimony. In the middle of her testimony, she apologized for something she had done to my older son. When my friend was trying to remind me of the girl's testimony, I remembered her telling her testimony, but I did not recall it being about my son. According to my friend, the girl had inadvertently confessed that she had molested my older son. As I listened to my friend, I thought, *It's good I did not hear her say that because if I had, I would have beat her up.*

After Antwon shared with me what he had witnessed and I had an opportunity to gather myself, we sat our sons down and talked to them, disciplined them, and prayed for them. From that point forward, we vowed to keep a closer watchful eye on them, realizing the abuse they had suffered was starting to show up in their behavior. I can't even begin to describe the pain my heart felt in that moment.

In one of my dreams, I was standing afar off, watching Antwon and his ex-fiancé pushing their daughter on a swing. When I awoke the next day, I pondered over the dream and its meaning. I had been feeling as though the two of them were very close, but I could never articulate exactly what I felt or believed about their relationship. I knew they had a connection, but they were clever about not revealing how deep the connection was. The dream clarified what I had come to believe about them. Lately, I began feeling that I was a rebound relationship and Antwon really wanted to be with his ex, and the dream was my confirmation. Little did I know that the truth of what was revealed in the dream would soon play out in real life.

In the midst of dealing with everyday life, I continued dealing with outside factors as well. Not surprisingly, my husband's ex-fiancé never stopped the constant calling. She was growing more and more frustrated with him for not paying child support. One day, she called and frustratingly left a message on the answering machine, saying his full name and asking when he was going to pay child support. Finally, Antwon called her back while we were in our bedroom. As he sat talking to her on the phone, I could hear the frustration in his voice. Wanting to alleviate the stress we were both feeling, I began to sing and pray, trying to take another approach to deal with her constant interruptions in our family life. He got up abruptly, walked into the hallway, and sat on the floor. Then, I heard him ask her, "What can I do to prove to you that I want to be there for my daughter?"

Unfortunately, Antwon did not agree with my tactic of trying to bring peace to the atmosphere. When he finished his phone call, he began yelling at me saying, "She knew you were here. You did not need to let it be known you are here!" I tried explaining that I wasn't trying to make my presence known to her, and I thought it was important to pray at that moment. His frustration towards me led me to being further frustrated to the point where I ended up going off on him in return.

From that point forward, our relationship became more and more volatile. I suggested we undergo marriage counseling, but Antwon never wanted to go. So, we carried on with what had become our normal behavior.

As one would expect, his daughter's mother was not happy about the reduction in her child support payments. In an attempt to reverse the decision that was made and to recoup the loss of funds, she called his phone incessantly. He would consistently ignore her calls, but she was not to be ignored. She would call until he answered, and in the interim, she would leave messages on our answering machine, stating his full legal name and threatening him with court. Eventually, we let her go ahead and file through the courts because we could no longer afford the $200 we were sending. When the court made its ruling, she ended up getting less than she originally was due to our financial hardship.

A year later, we were still at our new church, but we moved from the apartment into a townhouse. We enjoyed life off the island, and some of our friends would come visit, but due to the distance, the visits were very infrequent. We really only had each other, and to stay connected, I continued to call his job frequently throughout each work day, wanting to talk to him and hear his voice.

Eventually, I became pregnant with my fifth child about nine months after Joseph's death. During that pregnancy, I was very mean, acting out of character often. Due to losing my last child, I was shaky and paranoid during my pregnancy. I did not want to suffer another loss. I called one of the old associate pastors to let him know about my concerns about being pregnant. He shared his belief that I would not go through the same tragedy. I wasn't sure that his words were enough to assuage my fears, but it was an attempt.

In our townhouse, although the stairs were carpeted, they were very slippery. Antwon and I would fall constantly. During my pregnancy, I experienced at least one fall, and I thought my water had broken as a result, but I had actually only urinated. The realization caused me to laugh hysterically. The teenagers were there, and one of the girls asked if I was okay, but I was too busy laughing. My fall reminded us of when Antwon had fallen, causing us to laugh even harder. All we heard was "thump, thump, thump" as he fell. Then, at the end, he only said "ah." That was hilarious! Antwon was always so quiet, not talking much at all- even when he fell. And, when he did something out of character (such as falling or dancing) we would laugh because it was not like him at all. But, our laughter caused him to be more withdrawn. Because of his serious and quiet demeanor, I called him the fun-sucker sergeant. In contrast, I was the fun lively one, but we would both have a great time with the teenagers, who were coming over quite a bit.

On January 8, 2003, on my granny's birthday, I gave birth to our second daughter Tyliah Michelle Davis. I gave her my middle name, starting the trend of giving all my daughters (with exception to Tyonna) my mother's and my middle name- Michelle. Tyliah was an extremely beautiful baby. She looked like my side of the family and had a full head of hair. To me, she looked different from Tyonna and Joseph, and because of that everyone would say she was the mailman's baby- as a joke.

Not long after, my mother, my brother, who was about twenty-five and had received a record deal to rap with Wu-Tang, and my younger brother, who was about eight, came out to visit us. At that time, I did not embrace my older brother's lifestyle because I was not into the lifestyle he was living. I was pretty oblivious to it all because I was in my Christian world in my church, being sheltered from worldly living.

In 1997, I had gone home to California to visit, and my brother and I went to the grocery store in the Wu-Tang van. I didn't think much of it, but when we pulled up, everybody started staring and gathering around, trying to get a good look at my brother. I began asking people if they wanted his autograph. And, of course, they did. They wanted an autograph for themselves, and their mother, and their brother, and their sister, pretty much all their family members. My brother was annoyed with me for asking people if they wanted his autograph. He told me to stop asking, but I found the attention he was getting pretty cool.

Prior to that particular visit home, I had received a phone call from my best friend telling me my brother had signed a recording contract. She had seen him in the mall walking around with his friends, yelling Wu-Tang and acting like thuggish gangsters, proud to be newly signed artists. Once their first CD dropped, my mom sent me a copy. I listened to my brother rapping his lyrics for the first time, and I had tears in my eyes. His lyrics were crude, "I came out of my mother's womb with a blunt and a bloody dagger," but it was cool to hear him on a CD. Even after my friend told me the news of the recording contract and hearing the CD for myself, his level of fame did not register with me until I saw it up close and personal.

During my mother and brothers' visit with my family, my mother was happy to have our family together, and I was glad to have them with us as well although my relationship with my mother and brothers wasn't really that good, causing us not to speak very often. For one, my mother was always trying to run my life, and secondly, my older brother was the bully of the family. He spoke the way he wanted to speak, not caring if others found his speech or his attitude offensive.

While they were in town, our entire family went over to the island, and my brother had an opportunity to meet my friends and former pastors at a New Year's Eve service. I was excited to introduce them to my famous brother, but his fame was not a big deal to them. Like me, they were of a different mindset. As members of that church, we lived in isolation from what went on in the world at large as we kept our focus on God's Word. When my mom would call to tell me about things that were happening in the world, I would be surprised because I had turned a deaf ear to it all. At our church, it was frowned upon to listen to secular music, especially for the leaders. It was our regular practice to be in church all the time, so we did not focus on the world much.

As I stated earlier, many of the youth from our new church frequently visited our home and that continued throughout the duration of my mother and brothers' visit. On one particular day, one of the African pastor's daughters, who was in twelfth grade, was with my husband, my older brother and me riding around, looking for something to do. Unfortunately, Jersey did not have too much to offer in the form of entertainment. My brother, who was a lady's man, was riding in the back of the van with her. And, unbeknownst to Antwon and me, he was touching her in a sexually inappropriate manner. She did not tell me about the incident until later in life. When I learned about it, I felt very bad. If I had known, I would have protected her from my brother. Hearing her account of the incident reminded me of the dark secret of "touching" that haunted us.

On another day, during my mother and brothers' visit, my older brother was lying on the couch watching music videos. My mom told him she was sure I did not want him watching those videos around my children. Thankfully, he turned the channel. Later that night, I walked into the room where he was sleeping. To my surprise, he wasn't asleep at all. His eyes were moving rapidly to and fro. I asked if he was asleep. He said no, explaining he could not sleep because his mind was going nonstop, wandering all the time. Feeling his anguish and wondering what the problem was, I went upstairs and began to pray, crying out to the Lord for him. Later, I learned my brother was on drugs.

The next day, he had a belligerent tantrum. He was yelling and slamming cabinets, while my mom was in the background, telling him to shut up and be quiet. Antwon and I just sat there looking, taking everything in. My brother and I used to fight as teenagers, and I knew how callous he could be, so I did not want to get into a physical confrontation with him. That is why I sat there quietly as he went about as a storm throughout the house. However, I was disappointed in Antwon. I felt as the man of the house, he should have brought the situation under control. That was just another moment of disappointment in my husband, understanding he would not be a source of physical protection for me. After growing up with a brother who was aggressive and physical, that was what I was looking for in a man, someone who could and would protect me when I needed it.

Although my mother tried, she did not have control over the situation. Try as she might, she could not tame my brother. All the things she used to do to me when I was growing up did not work on my brother. He was not going for it. So, to keep peace in my home, my mother sent my brother back home on the bus. But, when he arrived back to California, he had nowhere to go because our stepfather did not like either of us, but he really had a strong disliking for my brother, and he did not want him in his home. My brother ended up staying with friends. A day later, he called and apologized to our mother.

After my mother and younger brother returned to California, not much later, we had another house guest. Antwon's younger brother came from Georgia with no specific time frame in mind for the length of his visit, and he ended up staying for six months, and I felt every day of it. During his stay with us, I became meaner. (Yes, I admit I was already a mean person.)

Have you heard the phrase, "The apple does not fall far from the tree"? Well, the phrase must unfortunately pertain to me because I began picking up my mother's character trait of being mean to my children, which was one thing I had vowed never to do. My sons were young, and they would behave like typical little boys, being mischievous. Instead of being patient with them, I would yell at them out of frustration as if they were adults. But, the yelling eventually escalated to being physical.

Once when my two sons were young, my oldest son, took a broom and swept it across my second son's face. I was horrified. I didn't know what he was thinking that would lead him to do that. But, I did not ask any questions. Before I knew it, I had lifted my hand and smacked him in the mouth, causing his lip to split and bleed. I immediately realized I had acted inappropriately. It was not right for me as an adult to exert my dominance over a child in that manner. From that point forward, I never behaved in that manner again.

When I had lived with my mother, she always exerted herself as the dominate one as the mother who was the authority in our relationship, making me understand I was the inferior one. In my relationship with my children, I understood as the dominate one- the mother- they only needed to listen to my instructions and follow them without being dealt with brutally. On my side, I needed understanding about the root of what I was going through and not take my frustrations out on my children and husband. After doing an in-depth evaluation of myself, my attitudes and behaviors, I realized that even though I was married, I was still empty. And, I did not know how to deal with that. I was having my fairytale life, but I was still very empty inside. I had ceased crying in the closet. I was not on welfare. I had received everything I had prayed for, yet I was still empty. As a result, I did not know how to deal with everything I was going through. So, I acted out. I was really mean in general, but especially to Antwon. From my perception, nothing he did was right. He irritated me at all times, and I was very unhappy.

Back to my brother-in-law and his visit. It seemed as though everything he did worked my nerves. For one, he was a drummer, and he drummed on any and everything he could, and his persistent beating irritated me to no end. Secondly, he was young and immature. His immaturity led him to have flings with many young girls rather than choosing one to have a relationship with. For example, he was messing around with one of the pastor's daughters, making me very upset. Then, he started messing around with other girls in the apartment complex we lived in.

Infuriating me even further, Antwon said nothing. He did not sit his brother down and give him words of advice, nothing. After some time, my brother-in-law and the pastor's son grew close and began hanging out in our home. They would goof off and keep up a bunch of nonsense. Just as all of his other activities, that was nerve wracking as well.

One day, Antwon, his brother, all the kids, and I were leaving home for an outing. When we pulled out of the garage, we did not wait until the door fully closed. We pulled out and headed to our destination. Unknowingly, before the garage door could go all the way down, the pastor's son slipped under the door and went into our home. One of our neighbors saw him slip inside and called us, to alert us of him being there. So, we turned around and went back. Sure enough, he was there. We asked what he was doing, and he said he saw the door was unlocked and he was going to lock it. Of course, his reasoning was a lie. We had not left a door unlocked. He only was able to gain entrance by slipping underneath the garage door as it closed. We informed our pastor about his son's activity, and he was embarrassed but not really surprised. Obviously, he was accustomed to his son being involved in underhanded activities but was really apologetic towards us.

Eventually, we decided to send Antwon's brother back to Georgia. He wasn't going to school nor was he working. He had just recently graduated high school and was about eighteen or nineteen years old, but he was not working on building a future for himself. So, we figured whatever he was doing in Jersey could be done in Georgia.

Not too much later, my world was turned upside down, when Antwon arrived home from work early one day with a box full of his belongings in his hand. He looked at me to answer the questions that covered my face. He said, "I was fired." The thought that came immediately to my mind was, "What are we going to do?"

As we pondered the situation, we truly did not know what to do, so we began to explore different avenues. The one thing we had going for us was Antwon was a veteran. That was something we could always fall back on.

I considered looking for a job, but I knew it was not a good idea because I would not bring in a much as my husband would. I could not contribute to the family as he could. Furthermore, I realized between the two of us, he was the smart one, and that caused me to have a complex and feel inadequate. But the reality was, he was better qualified to provide for the family than I was, and I accepted that.

Antwon was an aviation technician for the Navy. Normally, it would take two to three people to do his job, while he was able to maintain the responsibilities on his own. That's how smart he was. However, when he applied other places, he was found to be overqualified. That caused his job search to be rather difficult. When he considered going back to the military, he unfortunately could not get back in full time, but fortunately, he was able to re-enlist on a part-time basis. So, he was re-sworn in as a reservist two to three months after losing his job.

He was required to work one weekend a month, and he had to go back onto the island. Because he did not have living accommodations on the island, the military gave him a hotel room, and we moved there with him, after placing all of our household belongings in storage. Then, we packed up the van with our personal belongings and back to the island our family went. I was very disappointed and sad with the turn of events, and I really did not know what to expect next.

Reflections

Read the following questions, reflect upon your own life, and use this space as a private place to write.

Question 1- Have you ever learned something after the fact that you had no clue about? Share your experience.

_____

_____

_____

_____

_____

_____

_____

_____

_____

Question 2- How did you handle the situation?

_____

_____

_____

_____

_____

_____

_____

_____

_____

Question 3- Have you experienced the death of a loved one? If so, who was the person and what was the relationship of the person to you?

_____

_____

_____

Question 4- How did you cope with the death?

_____

_____

_____

_____

_____

_____

_____

Question 5- How do you cope with a fear?

_____

_____

_____

_____

_____

_____

_____

_____

4

Back on the Island
on Familiar Ground

After spending weeks in the hotel, we still did not have anywhere else to live, so Antwon's commander extended the hotel stay for one month. That gave us a bit of breathing room as far as accommodations were concerned, but we were still living day to day, trying to make ends meet. During that time, we began to attend our former church and fellowship with our pastors and church family. Although we were back in familiar territory at the church, the atmosphere did not seem quite the same.

Knowing our hotel stay would be soon coming to an end, I knew we needed to find somewhere to transition to, but we could not yet afford a place of our own. So, I began to consider which members of our church, if any, would be able to provide temporary housing for us. Taking into consideration the size of families and homes, I finally settled upon a sweet couple whom we had known prior to moving off the island. I suggested to Antwon that we should ask them. He agreed. Although the couple was friendly towards us, the wife did look a bit intimidating, but I decided to take the plunge and ask them if our family could stay with them for a while until we were able to move into a place of our own.

The couple was happy to welcome us into their home, and I breathed a sigh of relief in the midst of my surprise. I was reluctant to move in with anyone because I really did not desire to live with other people. I wanted us to have our own private accommodations, but our present circumstances did not allow for that to occur at that moment. Nevertheless, the wife was excited and very pleased that she and her husband could assist us in our time of need. They were very gracious to honor our request.

The couple lived alone with their adopted son in a large three-bedroom manufactured home out in the woods. Although they desired to have children of their own and had been trying for some time, their efforts had been unsuccessful, causing their third bedroom to be empty and available for us.

With their blessings, we moved in, and all six of us (my husband, me, and our four children) occupied the single bedroom. However, at times, we would spread out just to give each other some breathing space. Our two sons would sometimes camp out in the living room with their son, and on other occasions, Antwon, the girls, and I would sometimes sleep in the living room on the pull-out couch bed, leaving the bedroom for the boys to spread out and sleep comfortably.

All was well, and the arrangement worked nicely. Well... until it didn't. Until things took a turn for the worse, it was great to get to know the couple on an intimate level other than just attending church services and events together. In our free time, the wife and I would sit around and talk when she was off work. We would play Phase 10, and she would always beat my socks off.

We ending up being their house guests rent free for about six months to a year, and I was careful about us wearing out our welcome. My objective was to stay out of their way and to make my family's presence vaguely noticeable by keeping our area clean and by staying gone for long stretches of time during the day. We would come home at night to sleep and be gone again the next day.

That practice quickly backfired in my face. Instead of the couple appreciating their space and not bumping into us every time they turned around, they were offended by our absence. To them, it meant we did not really want to be in their home. So, they took that to mean we were using their home only as a place to sleep and that we really did not want to be around them. Ultimately, that was the beginning of tension in the home.

Secondly, the family had a cat that they loved, and we, on the other hand, were not cat people. We would hiss at the cat to get it to go away from us. The wife did not particularly care for us hissing at her pet and scaring it.

Thirdly, and probably the nail in our coffin, was the fact that the wife somehow began to believe she was pregnant. I'm not certain if her belief stemmed from ideas the pastor's wife was putting in her mind or how exactly she came to believe she was pregnant. All I know is out of nowhere, the pastor's wife kept saying the couple was believing for a baby and that they were walking by faith. Then, the wife began to feel flutters in her belly, and because she was a large woman, she appeared as though she could have been with child. However, I did not believe she was pregnant. She never directly stated her doctor had said she was pregnant, nor had she stated she had taken a pregnancy test that yielded a positive result. Yet, she believed she was pregnant. Even over the pulpit, the pastor and his wife kept saying the woman was pregnant by faith. I had doubts about the validity of her pregnancy the entire time. It wasn't that I didn't have faith as they did, but I just did not believe a child would be produced in her situation.

Somehow, she detected my unbelief, and with a microphone in her hand, she stated that she knew some people did not believe she would be having a baby. Then, she went one step further and said even people in her home did not believe and because of their unbelief, they could leave her home! Wow! That was a direct message to me and my family, and we heeded her words. At that point, the tension that had begun developing was at an all-time high. So, Antwon and I thought it would be best to prepare to move out.

Meanwhile, at church in our prayer room, many of the women placed padding on the floor, in preparation for the woman's delivery. Why she was going to give birth in the church instead of a hospital was also a mystery to me. To usher her delivery along, the other women began praying as if the woman was in labor. As I sat and watched what was taking place, I thought I was crazy for being the only one who did not believe she was pregnant. The women stayed in the prayer room for days, but no baby came.

Soon after, Antwon found another job for $15 an hour, but it was on the other side of the island. His traveling to work was more stress on the family, and it was not enough money to get us out of the hole we were in. Eventually, that caused more stress for us. Then finally, by the grace of God, a ram in the bush was delivered unto us.

Sadly, Antwon's aunt passed away, but she left him $15,000. We were both surprised because he had no clue she would be leaving him anything. Furthermore, we knew our family desperately needed the funds to catch up on past debts and to have a cushion for the months that lay ahead. His family, however, did not see things the way we did, which caused turmoil for us. They felt Antwon should have given them a portion of the money and also paid off his aunt's debts. In reality, the $15,000 would not stretch that far, and our current situation was our primary concern. With the position we were in, we needed all the money to give us a leg up. And it could not have come at a better time. It helped us in the nick of time to move from the couple's home into a three-bedroom condo.

Not long after our move, we learned we were pregnant again. Truthfully, it was one more thing to stress about. But at least we were in our own space, which afforded us privacy and our children could run around freely, as all children should have space to do.

About a year later, Antwon's grandfather passed away. Again, unexpectedly, Antwon was included in the will. That time, he inherited a van. Just like the money his aunt had bequeathed him in her will, the gift was right on time. We very much needed a second vehicle. At that point, our only mode of transportation was our van. However, instead of my husband keeping his grand-father's van, so the children and I could have a vehicle at our disposal while he was away at work with our van, he decided to give his grandfather's van to his brother. To say that I was angry with my husband's decision would be an understatement. I was completely livid. I felt as though my life was spiraling out of control, and from my perspective, my husband simply did not care about the condition of our family or our livelihood. His words may have said he cared, but his actions surely did not.

A few months later, we experienced the passing of my grandfather. So, my husband and I, along with our four children, loaded ourselves into our van and drove to California for the funeral services. Upon our arrival, we went to my grandmother's home, where we would be staying for the next week. My grandmother was still living in my childhood home. Although there was a lot of tumultuous activity in my life, I still felt as though I had everything going for me at that point. I was a married woman who was saved with a family that was complete with children.

At my church home, my husband and I had been elevated to the position of leaders, which was something that was not easy to attain because our pastors limited who would be given the responsibility to lead others. There were certain criteria one had to meet in order to be considered for leadership, and obviously Antwon and I had ticked all the boxes. Since we had returned to our church on the island, my husband and I had dedicated ourselves even more to the work of ministry, while staying focused on the Lord and continuing to build our faith. So, I really thought I had it going on. When I walked into my grandfather's funeral at a Baptist church with a red pantsuit on and the eyes of the church members were looking me up and down, I looked back at them as if to say, *What is your problem? There's nothing wrong with me. I have it going on.* In my mind, there was nothing anyone could say to me.

While we were visiting California, my older brother was incarcerated, and I paid him a visit after our grandfather's funeral. Sitting on the opposite side of the glass partition, I held up the obituary, so my brother could see it. He barely looked at it, while wearing a smirk on his face. Like me and our mother, he didn't deal with death well, and his look was more of a nervous gesture that attempted to mask his uncomfortableness. I guess it was a family thing. Instead of paying attention to the obituary, he was more interested in flirting with the women who walked by the glass partition. I know my brother wasn't happy about being behind bars, but I, on the other hand, was happy he was there because his containment kept him out of the rough street life that only led to trouble.

Also, while we were in town, we had an opportunity to visit my mother's church. Back home, my husband and I were part of the dance ministry at our church, and while at my mother's church, we had an opportunity to use our gifts and talents to dance during a worship service. Afterward, my mother's pastor prophesied into my life, telling me, "Girlfriend wants your man." I knew exactly who he was referring to when I heard his prophetic statement. He was talking about our pastor's oldest daughter. She and I had experienced a love-hate relationship due to her competitive spirit. While I was not in competition with her, I had come to later learn she was in competition with me. My mother's pastor was truly a blessing. Not only did he prophesy into my life, giving me a warning about the young girl's desire towards my husband, but he also gifted us with a monetary love offering. I was so pleased by how he was in tune with the Holy Spirit, who impressed upon him our financial need.

Eventually, the time arrived when we were scheduled to return home. So, we took the long drive back to Jersey where I was once again faced with our dire financial situation. There I was pregnant without the proper financial stability we needed. And things were growing increasingly worse.

To continue in the military reserves, my husband had to pass a PRT test (Physical Readiness Training test). Unfortunately, he did not have the physical endurance to successfully pass the test; therefore, he was going to be issued an honorable discharge. *That was the straw that broke the camel's back!* I did not know what to do as we were once again faced with a decrease in our income. I was so distraught and disappointed that all I could do was lie in bed day after day and cry uncontrollable tears.

One day as I lay in bed crying, my husband was in the shower praying. My tears were demonstrative of my continued belief that he did not care about the condition or wellbeing of our family. After he prayed, he shared with me his contrasting belief regarding his inability to pass the PRT. To him, God did not want him to continue in the military and supposedly that was why he did not pass the test. I vehemently disagreed with him, saying, "No, that's not God telling you that. That's your flesh. You don't care about the family, and you do not want to condition yourself to pass the test. That's just laziness on your part." Obviously, he did not like what I said to him because before I knew it, he had left the house.

I was left there with the children, so I got up to see what they were doing. I saw my son's backpack and began to look through it. I came across a pink slip. I didn't worry about looking to see whose name was on it because I knew it was about him. Lately, he had been acting out at school, was not completing all of his assignments, and was failing to apply himself. That had been going on for some time, and each time I received a complaint from his teacher, I threatened to spank him. As soon as I mentioned spanking him, he would start screaming, as if though I was causing him great pain when in reality, I had not even touched him yet. He would do that to deter me from following through with my threats. When I saw the pink slip, I began yelling at him, and as usual, he began screaming. That time he added in, "I'm sorry" and "I love you," but none of what he said was going to keep me away from him. So, I began spanking him as a means of disciplining him to let him know he needed to get his act together as it related to his studies.

Just before I had gone through his backpack, I had been waiting for one of my friends to come over and knock at the door. In the midst of dealing with my son, I heard a knock on the door, and I walked over to open it. To my surprise, it was not my friend. Instead, there were two police officers standing there. They said they were called because one of our neighbors heard screaming, and they were required to check the situation out. I said okay because I had nothing to hide.

While the officers were inside talking to my son, I called my husband at work and told him what was going on. We were laughing and joking about the situation, saying the police were making a big deal about my son receiving a spanking. Not too much later, other police officers arrived at my home. Shortly after that, even more officers showed up. At that point, I was really confused about what was going on. My laughter had ceased. The officers had begun taking pictures of my son, but I could not understand why. Then, my friend showed up right at that moment. After she came in, an officer asked me to step outside, so we could talk. I agreed and stepped outside. Then, the unexpected happened.

Reflections

Read the following questions, reflect upon your own life, and use this space as a private place to write.

Question 1- Have you ever heard from God regarding a specific situation? Do you believe you could have heard incorrectly due to wanting to handle the situation your own way?

_____

_____

_____

_____

_____

_____

_____

_____

Question 2- Have you ever felt as though God was taking too long to answer a question or concern you had?

_____

_____

_____

_____

_____

_____

_____

_____

Question 3- Have you or a loved one ever been in jail? If so, who was the person? Did you ever go and visit him/her? How was that experience for you?

_____

_____

_____

_____

_____

_____

Question 4- Which methods have you used to discipline your children? How effective were they?

_____

_____

_____

_____

_____

_____

_____

Question 5- Have you ever felt as though you should leave a specific job because you didn't like it? Did you actually do it? What was the outcome?

_____

_____

_____

_____

_____

_____

_____

Question 6- Are you the sole provider for your family? If so, have any of your financial decisions affected everyone?

_____

_____

_____

_____

_____

_____

_____

About the Author

Dr. LaMonica Abner's story began when she was Sister LaMonica Abner, the founder and CEO of the LaMonica Abner Ministries, out of which she still preaches to the lost and hurting, performs liturgical dances, and sponsors an annual Spiritual Warfare Conference. In 2024, it will be the tenth year of the Spiritual Warfare Conference.

Several years ago, Sis. Abner founded HELP (HE Lifts People); a ministry that caters to the needs of the homeless and elderly, and assists in making referrals for clothing, food, shelter, and personal care. Sister Abner grew up in a Christian family and was baptized as a child in a church where her grandmother was a member. Beyond those early years, her journey into Christian service actually began 24 years ago when Sister Abner had hands-on training in pulpit decorum and protocols, which enabled her to subsequently serve in administrative positions as an armor bearer and auxiliary leader wherever she was led to serve.

Sister Abner also has training in the proper use and adjustment of sound systems and microphones. Further, her training in flag and liturgical dancing, and designing of multimedia such as banners, pamphlets, and tracts, brought opportunities to participate in street, convalescent, and prison ministries outreach, and to minister in dramas, and with illustrative sermons for children's ministry.

In 2005 through 2006, not only did Sister Abner serve as armor bearer to First Lady Mensah, and as executive secretary to Pastor Obadyah Mensah of Resurrection Power International Ministries in Renton Washington, she also served there as Youth Pastor. Later on, in 2012, she served as armor bearer, dance leader, and trustee at the True Light Apostolic Ministry under Pastor and Mrs. Charles Travis in Adelanto, California.

It was in 2014 when Pastor Moses L. Collins, Jr. of Glory Bound Missionary Baptist Church in Compton, California, recognized Sis. Abner as a prophetess. It was shortly after this time that the LaMonica Abner Ministries and the subsequent Spiritual Warfare Conference were born. In 2016, though she had already suffered lifelong ridicule for having been homeless, surviving two divorces, and wrongfully enduring the loss of her children, Prophetess Abner found job success in the very area that was lacking in her life for so many years: *Security*. As destiny would have it, she rose to the rank of supervisor in security in less than a year, and temporarily worked in leadership security for Kaiser Permanente. She has since been promoted on a different job to Lead Field Manager where she oversees supervisors and is over 300 guards. Through it all, Prophetess Abner still follows the voice of God. Additionally, in 2016, Sis. Abner's first prayer CD was released. Since their inceptions, all these ministries have positively impacted many lives for the Kingdom of God.

Prophetess LaMonica Abner's continuing desire for the will of God to groom her spiritual deportment led her to the City of Refuge Church where she served under the tutelage of Bishop Noel Jones, and his staff of anointed instructors who engaged her in theological training and coursework for what was soon to be even greater ministry. Eventually leaving the City of Refuge, Prophetess Abner served under Bishop Marcus C. Fisher, Jr. and the Kingdom United Ministerial Alliance (KUMA), who ordained her as an Evangelist.

Under Bishop Fisher's leadership, Evangelist Abner served under two pastors: Overseer Tejanni Campbell of Garment of Praise Church, and Overseer Chuck Boom-Bryant of the Harvest Place Outreach Center, under whom Evangelist Abner was ordained as an associate pastor. Her countless life experiences and lessons are currently being compiled in her autobiography, *Beauty for Ashes, and* will be featured on Barnes and Noble

Bookstores and the Walk by Faith bookstores in Carson, California, this October, 2022. Other works by Evangelist Abner, including *A Book of Prayers* (a personal prayer book), *From the Pit to the Palace*, and a second prayer CD will soon be available in bookstores everywhere. In the meantime, an even greater assignment and challenge was on the horizon.

Evangelist Abner recalled that several years earlier, the Lord had spoken to her about starting her own church. But too afraid to step out and do it, she put if off. (Compelled by a deep conviction to obey God, however, her earnest prayer became, "Lord, deliver me from ME".) All glory and praise continue to go to God; for in August of 2020, two weeks after much prayer, Inner Healing International Ministries at Gonzales Park in Compton California was launched with a Monday night worship service. Within nearly three months of opening, IHIM's membership grew exponentially from three people (Evangelist Abner, a daughter, and a grandson), to approximately 40 people, and is still growing under the direction of the Holy Spirit.

Moving forward in the destiny designed for her life, on July 25, 2021, and in respect of her diligent work in ministry, the Board of Trustees at the Christ Is the Answer University in Opa-Locka Florida, conferred upon Pastor Abner the degree of Doctor of Theology, with a major in Religious Studies. And to add glory to praise, shortly thereafter on August 29, 2021, in the very park that is home to IHIM ministries, Dr. LaMonica Abner was officially installed as the Senior Pastor of Inner Healing International Ministries by Apostle Bryant-Boom, Overseer of Harvest Place Outreach Center, with laying on of hands by members of attending Presbytery.

From Sister, to Prophetess, to Evangelist, to Doctor and Senior Pastor: without a doubt, Dr. LaMonica Abner's many accomplishments and her spiritual gifts will always be used to advance the Kingdom of God wherever the Lord takes her. In light of it all, however, her ultimate goal is to someday hear the Lord say, "Well done, thou good and faithful servant..." (Matthew 25: 23).

Printed in the USA
CPSIA information can be obtained
at www.ICGtesting.com
LVHW011025101123
763015LV00031B/40

9 781945 102981